Hands-On STEM

FOCUS ON WAVES

by Cheryl Mansfield

FOCUS READERS

FOCUS READERS

www.focusreaders.com

Focus Readers is distributed by North Star Editions:
sales@northstareditions.com | 888-417-0195

Produced for Focus Readers by Red Line Editorial.

Content Consultant: Bruce Bolon, Associate Professor of Physics, Hamline University

Photographs ©: Alex Staroseltsev/Shutterstock Images, cover, 1; Jingjits Photography/Shutterstock Images, 4–5; Richinpit/iStockphoto, 7; damircudic/iStockphoto, 8–9; EvgeniiAnd/iStockphoto, 11; Fouad A. Saad/Shutterstock Images, 13; jamesbenet/iStockphoto, 15; Red Line Editorial, 17; PeopleImages/iStockphoto, 19; ArtwayPics/iStockphoto, 20–21; 3DSculptor/iStockphoto, 23, 29; Wavebreakmedia/iStockphoto, 25; bach005/iStockphoto, 27

ISBN
978-1-63517-287-4 (hardcover)
978-1-63517-352-9 (paperback)
978-1-63517-482-3 (ebook pdf)
978-1-63517-417-5 (hosted ebook)

Library of Congress Control Number: 2017935152

Printed in the United States of America
Mankato, MN
June, 2017

About the Author

Cheryl Mansfield was meant to write for kids. At age nine, she wrote her first nonfiction story. It was about lions. Everyone in her class read it.

TABLE OF CONTENTS

CHAPTER 1

A DAY AT THE BEACH

David is at the beach with his family. He runs to the shore. A small wave rolls onto his feet. Then he looks out at the ocean. He sees surfers riding large waves. What causes these waves to happen?

Ocean waves are often caused by wind.

Waves are regular **patterns** of motion. They are caused when an energy source creates a **disturbance**. This disturbance then travels. It carries energy from one place to another.

For waves on a lake, the energy source is usually the wind. The ripples on the surface are the disturbance. The disturbance carries the energy of the wave.

But waves are not only in water. They are everywhere in nature.

People find many ways to enjoy waves.

CHAPTER 2

WHAT IS A WAVE?

There are many types of waves in nature. One type is called mechanical waves. Another type is called electromagnetic waves.

Mechanical waves need the help of **matter** to make them move.

Sound waves allow people to hear. They are one example of mechanical waves.

Particles in matter bump into other particles. Energy is passed between particles as the wave travels. Ocean waves are one example of mechanical waves. Sound waves are another.

Electromagnetic waves are different from mechanical waves. They can travel without the help of matter. They can travel through space. Radio waves are one example of electromagnetic waves. Light waves are another. For

Visible light is one type of electromagnetic wave.

example, electromagnetic waves from the sun travel through space. They reach Earth even though there is very little matter in space.

Waves move in different ways. Some waves are known as transverse waves. In these waves, the wave travels in one direction. But the disturbance moves back and forth in a **perpendicular** direction. For example, suppose a transverse wave is traveling upward. The disturbance moves back and forth **horizontally**. Electromagnetic waves are one example of transverse waves.

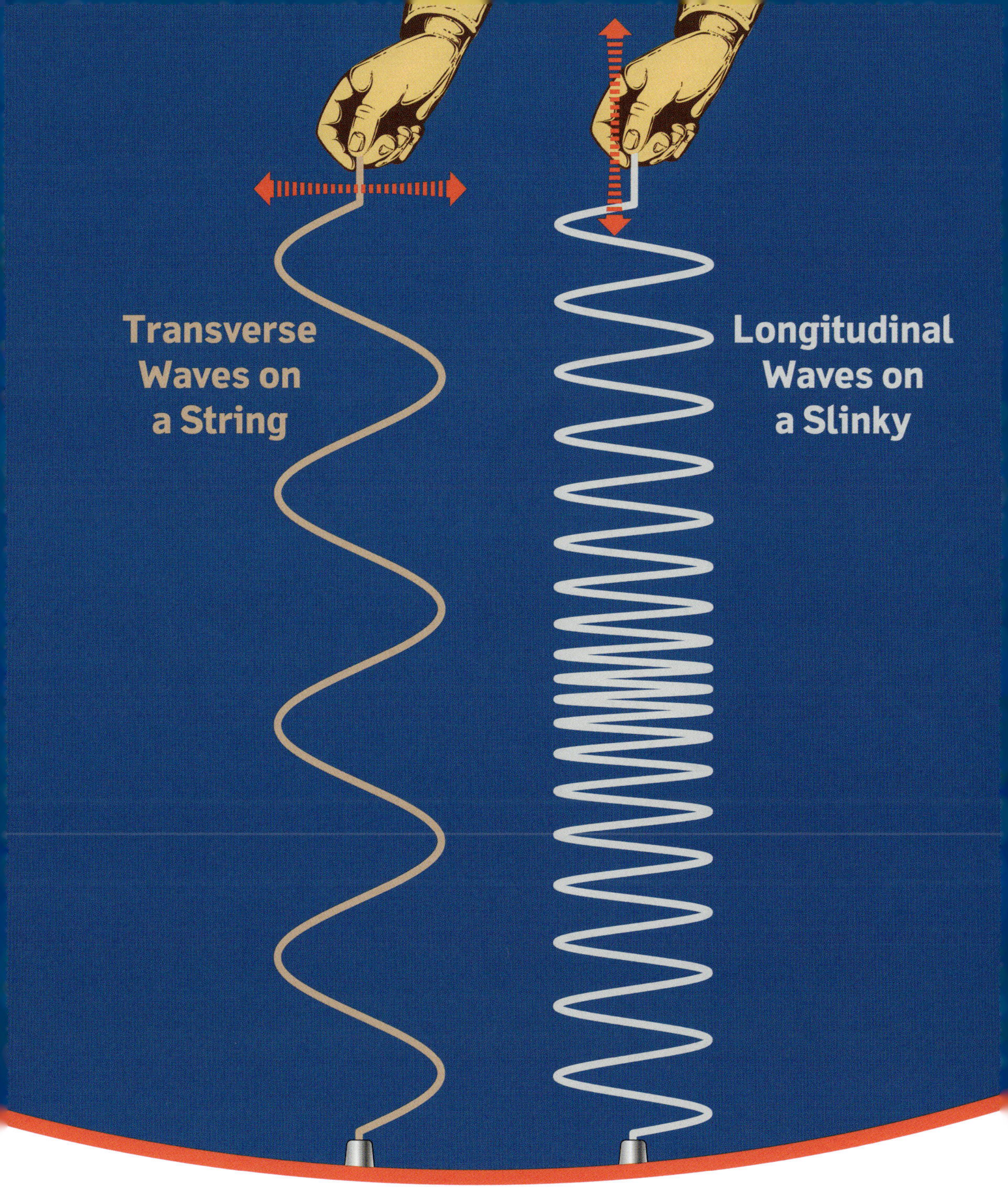

Waving a piece of string back and forth creates transverse waves. Pulling a Slinky up and down creates longitudinal waves.

Some waves move another way. In longitudinal waves, the disturbance moves back and forth in the same direction that the wave travels. Sound waves are an example. These waves travel through the air. They allow us to hear.

Water waves are more complicated. They involve both transverse and longitudinal motion. Imagine a leaf floating on the surface of a pond. When a wave

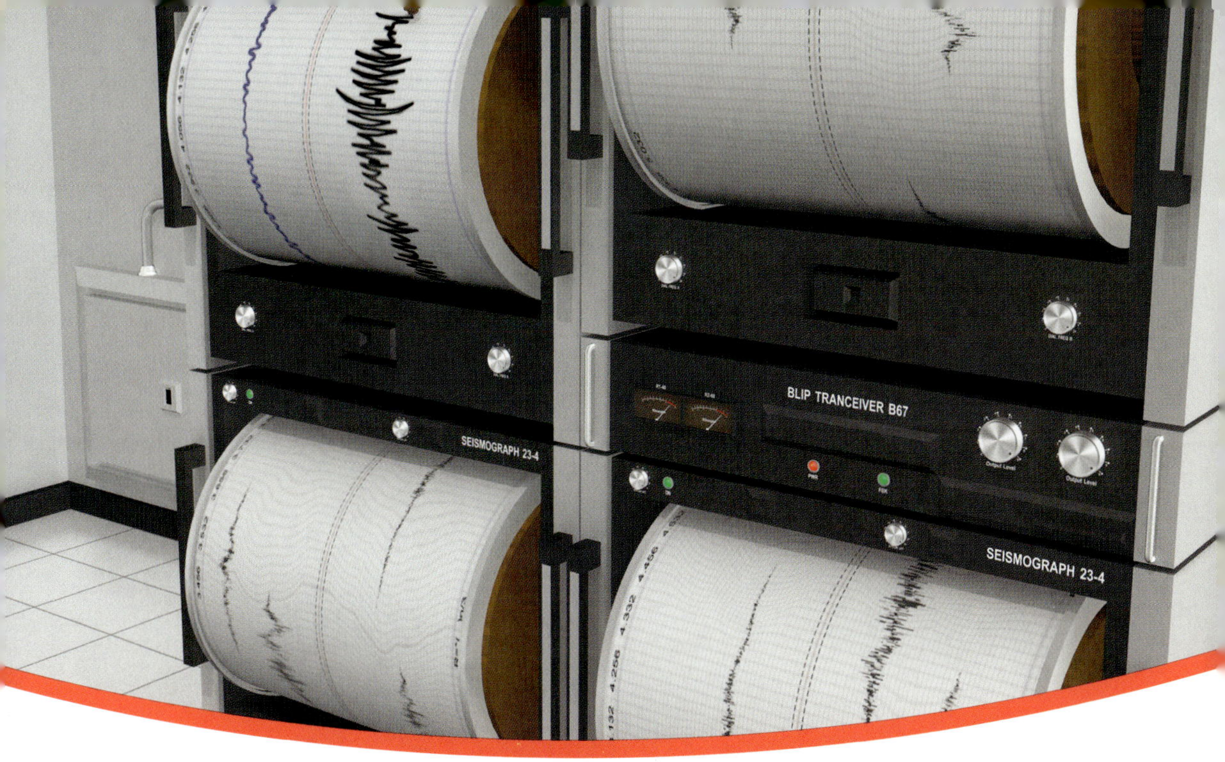

Scientists use a machine to measure waves that travel through Earth.

passes by, the leaf moves up and down. It also moves side to side.

Scientists measure waves in different ways. One measurement is called amplitude. This measures how large the disturbance is.

The amplitude of a wave is related to the wave's energy. For water waves, the top of the wave is called the crest. The bottom of the wave is called the trough. The amplitude measures how high the crest is compared to the water level. The amplitude also measures how low the trough is. Some waves have low energy, such as small ripples on a pond. Other waves have high energy, such as large waves on the ocean.

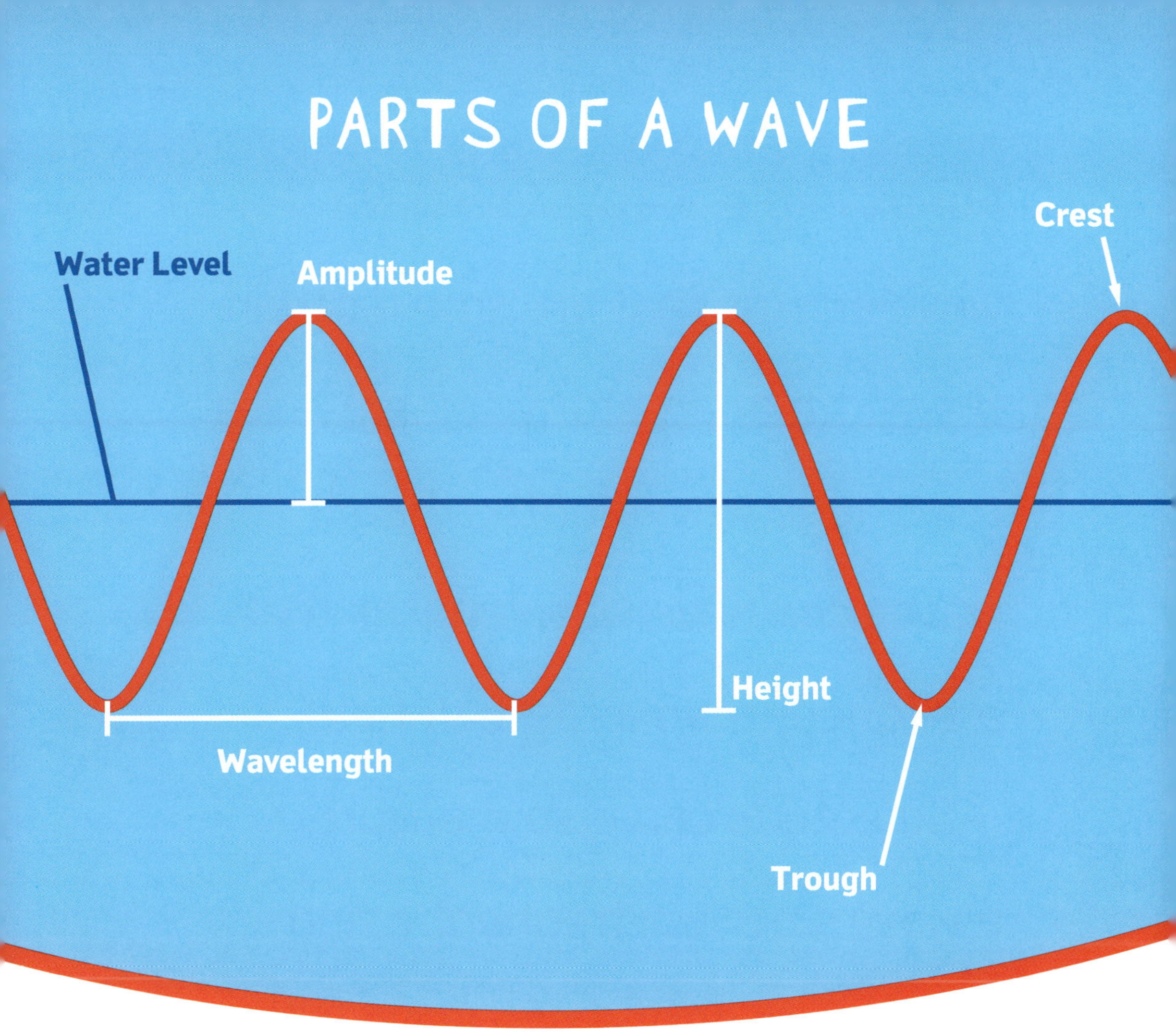

Wavelength is another measurement. It tells the length of one complete cycle of a wave. Some waves have tiny wavelengths.

For example, X-rays can have wavelengths that are smaller than the width of an **atom**. Other waves have huge wavelengths. Radio waves can have wavelengths that are longer than a football field.

Scientists can also measure a wave's period, frequency, and speed. The period of a wave is the amount of time it takes to complete one cycle. The frequency is the number of cycles passing by a point

Radio waves have low frequencies compared to other electromagnetic waves.

every second. The speed of the wave is how fast it travels.

CHAPTER 3

WAVES IN THE REAL WORLD

Waves are all around us. Many of them are helpful, but some can be harmful. Earthquakes involve waves inside Earth. These waves cause the ground to tremble. This can destroy buildings.

A 2011 earthquake in Japan caused major destruction.

Tsunamis can be harmful, too. These huge ocean waves can cause major damage.

Some waves are very useful. For example, we use radio waves to send information. These waves are a type of electromagnetic wave. They are used in cell phones and TVs. They are used with **satellites**, too.

People also use waves to cook. Microwaves are another type of electromagnetic wave. The waves

Satellites send information around the world using electromagnetic waves.

in a microwave oven heat the water in food. This causes the food to get warmer.

Waves are important in hospitals as well. For example, doctors use X-rays. This is another type of electromagnetic wave. X-rays can pass easily through skin but not very easily through bone. X-rays let doctors see inside our bodies.

And without waves, we would not be able to see. Light waves bounce off objects. Then the waves go into our eyes. This allows us to see. We use waves every day!

People use light waves when they read books.

SCIENCE IN ACTION!

WAVES WITH A SLINKY

Can you make waves with a Slinky? Perform this experiment to find out.

Step 1: Ask a friend to hold one end of the Slinky on the floor. Keep it still.

Step 2: Hold the other end of the Slinky in your hand. Make sure it is directly above the bottom end.

Step 3: Quickly move your end of the Slinky left and right.

In which direction do the waves move? Are these waves transverse or longitudinal? How could you make the other type of wave?

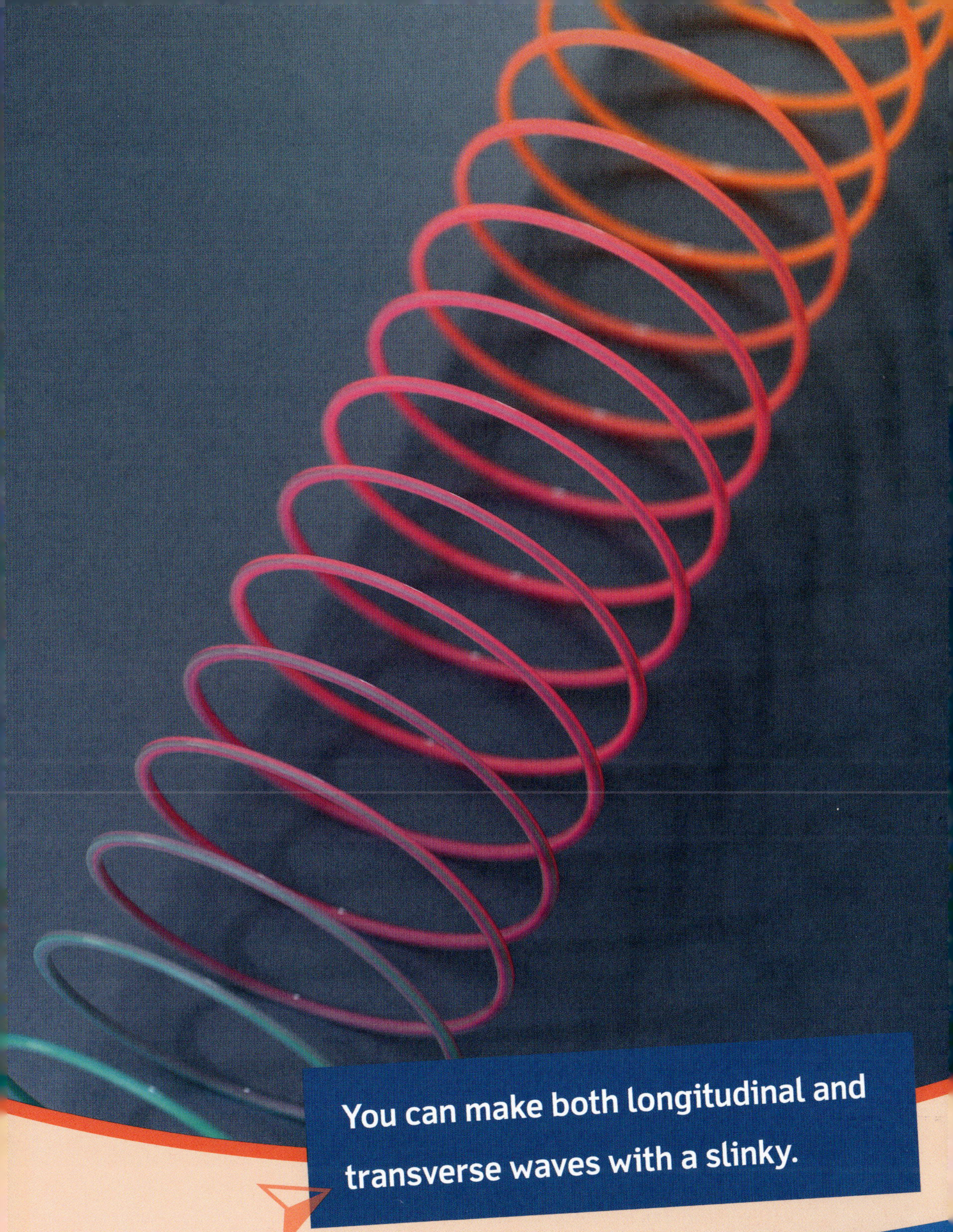

You can make both longitudinal and transverse waves with a slinky.

FOCUS ON

WAVES

Write your answers on a separate piece of paper.

1. Write a paragraph that describes the main ideas of Chapter 2.
2. Which kind of wave do you think would be most difficult to live without? Why?
3. Which of these three waves can have wavelengths that are smaller than the width of an atom?
    - A. radio waves
    - B. light waves
    - C. X-rays
4. A microwave is which of the following?
    - A. longitudinal wave
    - B. mechanical wave
    - C. transverse wave

5. What does **ripples** mean in this book?

For waves on a lake, the energy source is usually the wind. The ***ripples*** *on the surface are the disturbance.*

A. sources of energy
B. small waves
C. speed of wind

6. What does **tremble** mean in this book?

Earthquakes involve waves inside Earth. These waves cause the ground to ***tremble****.*

A. to shake
B. to flip
C. to burn

Answer key on page 32.

GLOSSARY

atom
A small unit of matter that most of the objects around us are made of.

disturbance
The thing that carries energy as a wave travels.

horizontally
In a way that is parallel to the ground.

matter
Anything that takes up space.

patterns
Things that repeat regularly.

perpendicular
At a 90-degree angle with another surface.

satellites
Objects in space that travel around much larger objects.

TO LEARN MORE

BOOKS

Hudak, Heather C. *What Are Waves?* New York: Crabtree, 2017.

Ivancic, Linda. *What Is a Wave?* New York: Cavendish Square, 2016.

Rowell, Rebecca. *Energy and Waves through Infographics*. Minneapolis: Lerner Publications, 2014.

NOTE TO EDUCATORS

Visit **www.focusreaders.com** to find lesson plans, activities, links, and other resources related to this title.

INDEX

Answer Key: 1. Answers will vary; **2.** Answers will vary; **3.** C; **4.** C; **5.** B; **6.** A